THIS JOURNAL BELONGS TO:

DATE:

Delight thyself also in the LORD: and he shall give thee the desires of thine heart. Psalm 37:4

Pleasant words are as an honeycomb, sweet to the soul, and health to the bones. Proverbs 16:24

Trust in the LORD with all thine heart; and lean not unto thine own understanding. Proverbs 3:5

In all thy ways acknowledge him, and he shall direct thy paths. Proverbs 3:6

The effectual fervent prayer of a righteous man availeth much. James 5:16

And we know that all things work together for good to them that love God,
to them who are the called according to his purpose. Romans 8:28

I will bless the LORD at all times: his praise shall continually be in my mouth. Psalm 34:1

Delight thyself also in the LORD: and he shall give thee the desires of thine heart. Psalm 37:4

Pleasant words are as an honeycomb, sweet to the soul, and health to the bones. Proverbs 16:24

Trust in the LORD with all thine heart; and lean not unto thine own understanding. Proverbs 3:5

In all thy ways acknowledge him, and he shall direct thy paths. Proverbs 3:6

The effectual fervent prayer of a righteous man availeth much. James 5:16

I can do all things through Christ which strengtheneth me. Philippians 4:13

And we know that all things work together for good to them that love God,
to them who are the called according to his purpose. Romans 8:28

I will bless the LORD at all times: his praise shall continually be in my mouth. Psalm 34:1

Delight thyself also in the LORD: and he shall give thee the desires of thine heart. Psalm 37:4

Pleasant words are as an honeycomb, sweet to the soul, and health to the bones. Proverbs 16:24

Trust in the LORD with all thine heart; and lean not unto thine own understanding. Proverbs 3:5

In all thy ways acknowledge him, and he shall direct thy paths. Proverbs 3:6

The effectual fervent prayer of a righteous man availeth much. James 5:16

I can do all things through Christ which strengtheneth me. Philippians 4:13

And we know that all things work together for good to them that love God,
to them who are the called according to his purpose. Romans 8:28

I will bless the LORD at all times: his praise shall continually be in my mouth. Psalm 34:1

Delight thyself also in the LORD: and he shall give thee the desires of thine heart. Psalm 37:4

Pleasant words are as an honeycomb, sweet to the soul, and health to the bones. Proverbs 16:24

Trust in the LORD with all thine heart; and lean not unto thine own understanding. Proverbs 3:5

In all thy ways acknowledge him, and he shall direct thy paths. Proverbs 3:6

The effectual fervent prayer of a righteous man availeth much. James 5:16

I can do all things through Christ which strengtheneth me. Philippians 4:13

And we know that all things work together for good to them that love God,
to them who are the called according to his purpose. Romans 8:28

I will bless the LORD at all times: his praise shall continually be in my mouth. Psalm 34:1

Delight thyself also in the LORD: and he shall give thee the desires of thine heart. Psalm 37:4

Pleasant words are as an honeycomb, sweet to the soul, and health to the bones. Proverbs 16:24

Trust in the LORD with all thine heart; and lean not unto thine own understanding. Proverbs 3:5

In all thy ways acknowledge him, and he shall direct thy paths. Proverbs 3:6

The effectual fervent prayer of a righteous man availeth much. James 5:16

I can do all things through Christ which strengtheneth me. Philippians 4:13

And we know that all things work together for good to them that love God,
to them who are the called according to his purpose. Romans 8:28

I will bless the LORD at all times: his praise shall continually be in my mouth. Psalm 34:1

Delight thyself also in the LORD: and he shall give thee the desires of thine heart. Psalm 37:4

Pleasant words are as an honeycomb, sweet to the soul, and health to the bones. Proverbs 16:24

Trust in the LORD with all thine heart; and lean not unto thine own understanding. Proverbs 3:5

In all thy ways acknowledge him, and he shall direct thy paths. Proverbs 3:6

The effectual fervent prayer of a righteous man availeth much. James 5:16

I can do all things through Christ which strengtheneth me. Philippians 4:13

And we know that all things work together for good to them that love God,
to them who are the called according to his purpose. Romans 8:28

I will bless the LORD at all times: his praise shall continually be in my mouth. Psalm 34:1

Delight thyself also in the LORD: and he shall give thee the desires of thine heart. Psalm 37:4

Pleasant words are as an honeycomb, sweet to the soul, and health to the bones. Proverbs 16:24

Trust in the LORD with all thine heart; and lean not unto thine own understanding. Proverbs 3:5

In all thy ways acknowledge him, and he shall direct thy paths. Proverbs 3:6

The effectual fervent prayer of a righteous man availeth much. James 5:16

I can do all things through Christ which strengtheneth me. Philippians 4:13

And we know that all things work together for good to them that love God,
to them who are the called according to his purpose. Romans 8:28

I will bless the LORD at all times: his praise shall continually be in my mouth. Psalm 34:1

Delight thyself also in the LORD: and he shall give thee the desires of thine heart. Psalm 37:4

Pleasant words are as an honeycomb, sweet to the soul, and health to the bones. Proverbs 16:24

Trust in the LORD with all thine heart; and lean not unto thine own understanding. Proverbs 3:5

In all thy ways acknowledge him, and he shall direct thy paths. Proverbs 3:6

The effectual fervent prayer of a righteous man availeth much. James 5:16

I can do all things through Christ which strengtheneth me. Philippians 4:13

And we know that all things work together for good to them that love God,
to them who are the called according to his purpose. Romans 8:28

I will bless the LORD at all times: his praise shall continually be in my mouth. Psalm 34:1

Delight thyself also in the LORD: and he shall give thee the desires of thine heart. Psalm 37:4

Pleasant words are as an honeycomb, sweet to the soul, and health to the bones. Proverbs 16:24

Trust in the LORD with all thine heart; and lean not unto thine own understanding. Proverbs 3:5

In all thy ways acknowledge him, and he shall direct thy paths. Proverbs 3:6

The effectual fervent prayer of a righteous man availeth much. James 5:16

I can do all things through Christ which strengtheneth me. Philippians 4:13

And we know that all things work together for good to them that love God,
to them who are the called according to his purpose. Romans 8:28

I will bless the LORD at all times: his praise shall continually be in my mouth. Psalm 34:1

Delight thyself also in the LORD: and he shall give thee the desires of thine heart. Psalm 37:4

Pleasant words are as an honeycomb, sweet to the soul, and health to the bones. Proverbs 16:24

Trust in the LORD with all thine heart; and lean not unto thine own understanding. Proverbs 3:5

In all thy ways acknowledge him, and he shall direct thy paths. Proverbs 3:6

The effectual fervent prayer of a righteous man availeth much. James 5:16

I can do all things through Christ which strengtheneth me. Philippians 4:13

And we know that all things work together for good to them that love God,
to them who are the called according to his purpose. Romans 8:28

I will bless the LORD at all times: his praise shall continually be in my mouth. Psalm 34:1

Delight thyself also in the LORD: and he shall give thee the desires of thine heart. Psalm 37:4

Pleasant words are as an honeycomb, sweet to the soul, and health to the bones. Proverbs 16:24

Trust in the LORD with all thine heart; and lean not unto thine own understanding. Proverbs 3:5

In all thy ways acknowledge him, and he shall direct thy paths. Proverbs 3:6

The effectual fervent prayer of a righteous man availeth much. James 5:16

I can do all things through Christ which strengtheneth me. Philippians 4:13

And we know that all things work together for good to them that love God,
to them who are the called according to his purpose. Romans 8:28

I will bless the LORD at all times: his praise shall continually be in my mouth. Psalm 34:1

Delight thyself also in the LORD: and he shall give thee the desires of thine heart. Psalm 37:4

Pleasant words are as an honeycomb, sweet to the soul, and health to the bones. Proverbs 16:24

Trust in the LORD with all thine heart; and lean not unto thine own understanding. Proverbs 3:5

In all thy ways acknowledge him, and he shall direct thy paths. Proverbs 3:6

The effectual fervent prayer of a righteous man availeth much. James 5:16

I can do all things through Christ which strengtheneth me. Philippians 4:13

And we know that all things work together for good to them that love God,
to them who are the called according to his purpose. Romans 8:28

I will bless the LORD at all times: his praise shall continually be in my mouth. Psalm 34:1

Delight thyself also in the LORD: and he shall give thee the desires of thine heart. Psalm 37:4

Pleasant words are as an honeycomb, sweet to the soul, and health to the bones. Proverbs 16:24

Trust in the LORD with all thine heart; and lean not unto thine own understanding. Proverbs 3:5

In all thy ways acknowledge him, and he shall direct thy paths. Proverbs 3:6

The effectual fervent prayer of a righteous man availeth much. James 5:16

I can do all things through Christ which strengtheneth me. Philippians 4:13

And we know that all things work together for good to them that love God,
to them who are the called according to his purpose. Romans 8:28

I will bless the LORD at all times: his praise shall continually be in my mouth. Psalm 34:1

Delight thyself also in the LORD: and he shall give thee the desires of thine heart. Psalm 37:4

Pleasant words are as an honeycomb, sweet to the soul, and health to the bones. Proverbs 16:24

Trust in the LORD with all thine heart; and lean not unto thine own understanding. Proverbs 3:5

In all thy ways acknowledge him, and he shall direct thy paths. Proverbs 3:6

The effectual fervent prayer of a righteous man availeth much. James 5:16

I can do all things through Christ which strengtheneth me. Philippians 4:13

*And we know that all things work together for good to them that love God,
to them who are the called according to his purpose. Romans 8:28*

I will bless the LORD at all times: his praise shall continually be in my mouth. Psalm 34:1

Delight thyself also in the LORD: and he shall give thee the desires of thine heart. Psalm 37:4

Pleasant words are as an honeycomb, sweet to the soul, and health to the bones. Proverbs 16:24

Trust in the LORD with all thine heart; and lean not unto thine own understanding. Proverbs 3:5

In all thy ways acknowledge him, and he shall direct thy paths. Proverbs 3:6

The effectual fervent prayer of a righteous man availeth much. James 5:16

I can do all things through Christ which strengtheneth me. Philippians 4:13

And we know that all things work together for good to them that love God,
to them who are the called according to his purpose. Romans 8:28

I will bless the LORD at all times: his praise shall continually be in my mouth. Psalm 34:1

Delight thyself also in the LORD: and he shall give thee the desires of thine heart. Psalm 37:4

Pleasant words are as an honeycomb, sweet to the soul, and health to the bones. Proverbs 16:24

Trust in the LORD with all thine heart; and lean not unto thine own understanding. Proverbs 3:5

In all thy ways acknowledge him, and he shall direct thy paths. Proverbs 3:6

The effectual fervent prayer of a righteous man availeth much. James 5:16

I can do all things through Christ which strengtheneth me. Philippians 4:13

And we know that all things work together for good to them that love God,
to them who are the called according to his purpose. Romans 8:28

I will bless the LORD at all times: his praise shall continually be in my mouth. Psalm 34:1